38

MIKI DEVIVO

Copyright © 2016 by Story Bridge Media LLC
Miki DeVivo

All rights reserved. This book or any portion thereof may not be reproduced or used in any manner whatsoever without the express written permission of the publisher except for the use of brief quotations in a book review.

Printed in the United States of America

First Printing, 2016

ISBN 978-0-9984388-0-1
www.mikidevivo.com

Design
Sutton Long
www.suttonlong.com

DEDICATION

To Joe, for staying
and teaching me how to stay.

To Renée and Max, for being
and teaching me how to be.

To Kiki, for seeing
and teaching me how it feels to be seen.

And to Ron, for hurting
and teaching me how to heal.

TABLE OF CONTENTS

Introduction 7
Between Us 9
The Things I Didn't Know 10
Not A Father 13
Bully 16
What Have I Forgotten 18
Instantly 20
Big Now 22
Outside 24
The Size of Love 26
The Tide of Her 28
Almost Decadent 30
With A Capital "A" 34
Enough 37
Math Problem 40
Surrender 43
Learning to Stay 47
Twenty Years 50
My Job 53
Already Forgiven 56
Evidence 58
Christmas Morning 62
It Looks Nothing Like I Thought It Would 65
Growing Up 70
Hold Us Both 73
Good 76
Through Line 79
What Works 81
Quiet 83
Elemental 85
Hairbrush 87
One Thin Arm 90
Practice 93
Half 96
Name It 98
Magic 100
Mostly OK 102
For Sure 104
No Other Shoe 106
Afterward 108

September 29, 2012

INTRODUCTION

In a very real way, the act of writing the words in this book changed me. I'd sit down to write feeling and knowing one thing about myself and my life, and get up from the page feeling and knowing something new. The process helped me discover new meaning for old events, new perspective on old patterns, balm for old hurts.

In these poems I tell my truth about growing up with an emotionally abusive father. These poems are the first place I was able to name what happened for what it was, and as I wrote, I came to know that I have broken the cycle.

In these poems I tell my truth about marriage. How it looks nothing like the movies. How I learned to ask for help. How I stopped looking to be rescued and learned to love the realness of it.

In these poems I tell my truth about the hard days of motherhood. All the weight of it. The quiet joy, the tender bursting love. The messy wonderful hope of it.

And these photographs were my mindfulness practice, looking for evidence of love and beauty even in the midst of the chaos.

This book is about naming the things I couldn't name before, and the freedom to say out loud what had to be kept silent for so many years — telling the truth about the shadows, and coming to know that underneath it all is love.

As you read these poems, I hope they help you name something you've felt but never been able to put into words. I hope they bring you comfort. I hope they bring you peace. I hope you know you are not alone.

August 8, 2015

BETWEEN US

Remember:
the space between us
is a prayer,
not a rebuke.
Holy,
not a criticism.

THE THINGS I DIDN'T KNOW

No one told me parenthood would break me.
Beat me down with its impossibility.
Dismantle me.
No one told me I'd be flattened
and laid bare
by the unrelenting always never not of it.
Flayed open even as I carried a child's full weight on my heart.

No one told me there wouldn't be even one moment to stop.
Impossible to get up again
and again
and again,
and yet somehow to get up again anyway.
No one told me how to survive it.
How to pull myself back to myself.

No one told me my kid would be born
perfectly designed
to fit into the tender wounds
I thought had scabbed over.
No one told me that a gaslight burns just as deeply as a belt.
No one told me how to protect her from the anger I inherited.
No one told me how to heal the child in my heart
even as I raise the child of my body.

No one told me I would resent my husband.
Not in the 80s sitcom "you did this to me" way,
but in the "I'm drowning and you can't save me" way.

Sure they told me to ask for help.
But no one told me how to form the words
as I choked on panic.
How to form the words
when I didn't believe I deserved them.
How to form the words
when I didn't know the sound of my own voice.
They did tell me how easy love is supposed to be,
how soulmates *just happen*,
how The One will *just know* what you need without you saying a word.

But no one told me this Love Story is bullshit.
No one told me how to stay.
Leaving is glorified.
The spouse is always greener on the other side.
No one told me how you stay
when the only thing keeping you married
is the fact that you're married.

No one told me about the terror of becoming a mother
before you decide you want to be.
How it feels to be the only one you know drowning.
They didn't tell me how lonely it is.
Wondering if you're the only one.

No one told me the terror of not knowing what to do
and not knowing what to do
and not knowing what to do.
When every cry cuts through me
and sounds like *you're a failure you're a failure you're a failure.*

And you watch videos of when they were small and regret
time passed you by through a fog of anxiety.
You weren't all there.

And they didn't tell me how the years pass
and you bring yourself back together,
but the pieces are are bent and frayed at the end
and fit in different places.
One piece lost behind the bookcase.
One piece lost beneath the piano.

And you learn to say to your husband, "I need help,"
and you learn to receive
and you learn the sound of your own voice
and you get through.

And they didn't tell me I'd learn to stay.
I'd learn to do it again,
just one more time
and one more time
and one more time.

July 13, 2011

NOT A FATHER

I asked you not to call me.
You called me a bitch
and threatened to kill yourself.

You keep calling despite my request.
You show no tenderness,
no concern,
no care.
Either you mean it,
or you don't.
Either way
someone who uses threats
as love
is not a father.
That is not love.

You are consistent.
Never once
have you reached out with concern,
shared a desire to know me,
or shown remorse.
You've never said you miss me.

When you say, "My daughter won't talk to me,"
I become the bad guy,
you the innocent.
"How did this happen?"

Let me tell you,
It was not easy
to decide I was better off without you.
I would rather have a dad.
But I couldn't anymore.
You had twenty four years to change.
I will not give you any more time.

I've changed.
I heard your rage
speak through my mouth,

your desire to control
rise in my body.

I hurt my children.
And I stopped.
I refuse to let it be ok.
I refuse to let it be normal.
I refuse to treat my children
the way you treated me.

Even if I'm wrong,
and I'm the bad guy,
your behavior since is wrong.
If you don't mean it,
I don't believe you.
You've never behaved any differently.
Or you mean every word,
and you're right,
I won't talk to you
and you deserve to be alone.

October 24, 2012

BULLY

My mother served him the papers when I was five.
She gave herself, gave him five years of my life.
If it wasn't ok by then, she'd go.
Not for her.
She was already fifteen years in by then.

Six-year-old me doesn't really remember much.
She remembers moving away from him.
And then moving back in with him.
The judge made my mother "give it one more try."

How to explain it to a child?
When I knew I was going to become a mother
I had to decide
how to explain the absence
of someone still alive
but no longer welcome.
I didn't want my daughter to feel scared,
to think dads were capable of not loving their children.
I didn't want her to think his disease was something one of us could catch.

It came down to trust.
He does not deserve our trust.
He did not keep us safe.
He did not keep his word.
He made one choice.
We make a different one.
My daughter asks me if I'd ever been bullied.
I say no.
But I was wrong.
The word bully fits.
She knows what it means.
He was a bully.
So I tell her yes, I have.

We stayed for as long as we could.
My mom left when I was five.
I left when I was twenty four.
Because we trust ourselves.

December 15, 2012

WHAT HAVE I FORGOTTEN

They say amnesia is a common side effect of gaslighting.
When you can't trust your reality,
how can you be expected to remember it?
What I do remember
is my mom.
Always there.
Was then.
Now still.
Always there for me.
A constant constant.
Unwavering.

I know someday she will pass from this earth.
There will be things about her I will start to forget,
but never forget the way it felt—feels—
to be loved by her so completely.
Her imperfections make her all the more trustworthy.
She works her ass off to do right by me.

What have I forgotten of the first years of my children's lives?
I haven't forgotten the ways I have failed.
Times when my anger from the past
spilled out into the present
and I let my hand fly.
I work to remember to pause now when my anger flares.
Make a different choice.
I remember the moments when I failed.
But my heart deeply hopes they have forgotten.
I hope when they remember their beginning years
they feel my presence, my constant love.

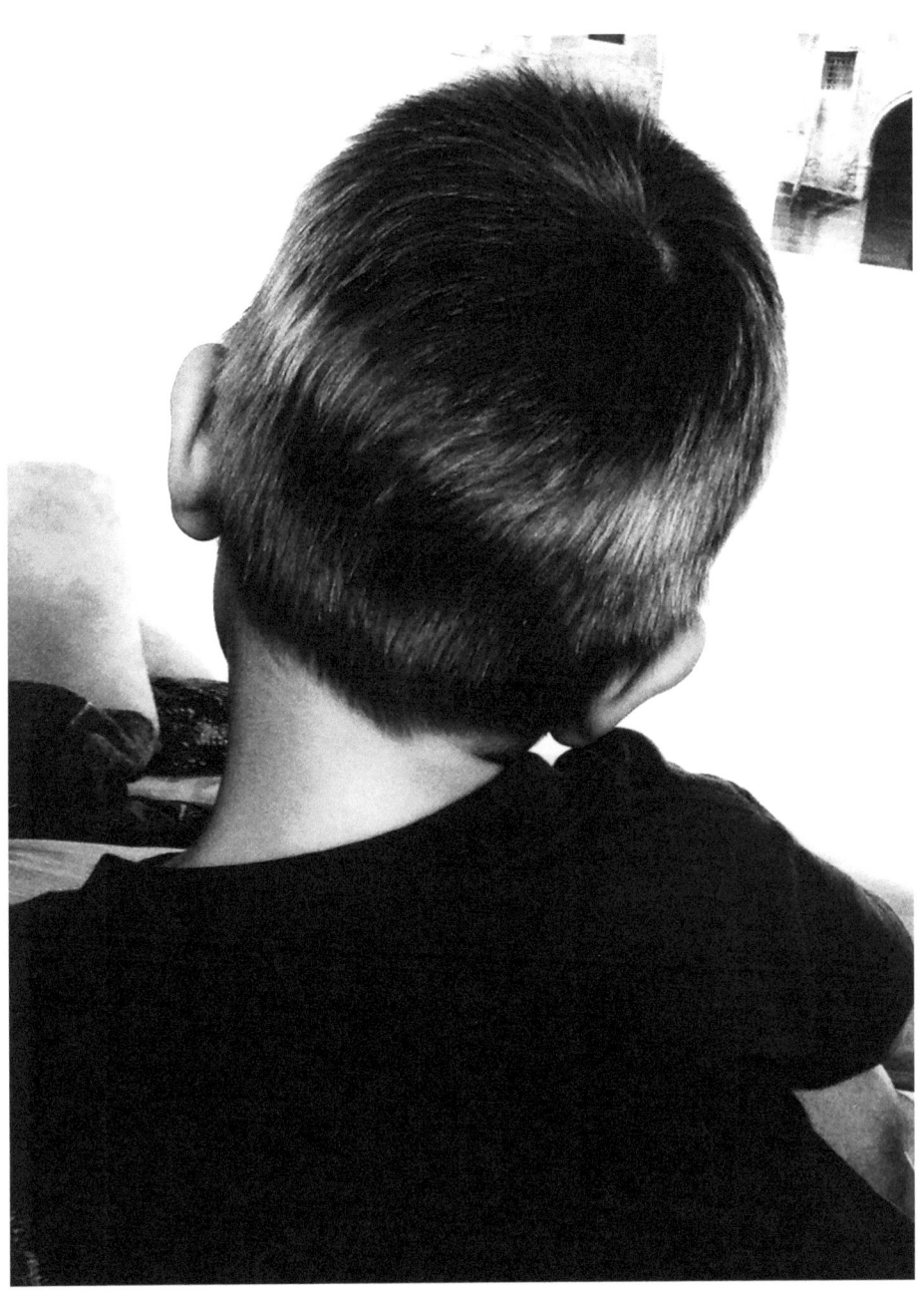

August 13, 2011

INSTANTLY

Things go sideways instantly.
I wait for the other shoe to drop.
I should be able to keep her calm.
I should be able to navigate it better
when she does get angry.
I should be able to turn it around.
It's my job as a parent to manage and control my kids
and I can't.
I worry it's my fault.
If I could be a better mother,
this wouldn't happen.

When my daughter's anger wells up
and things feel out of control
I feel the same panic wash over me.
I have to get away
and yet cannot move.
Blood courses fast through my belly and arms and fists.
Ears rush.
Vision blurs.
Part of my brain screams to lash out.
Lash back. Make it stop. Be bigger than. Be powerful over.
I doubt myself instantly.
I should spend more time with them.
They should have my full attention at all times.
I should always be available.
I should plan outings
and creative projects
and always say yes when they ask me to play.
If attention equals love then more attention equals more love.
And I am failing.

I worry they won't feel loved enough by me.
The books say it's all on me.
So many ways to fail.
I can never do enough.
I always fall short.
I fall, I fail, instantly.

March 6, 2016

BIG NOW

Today he is seven.
His hands small,
the distance between fingertip and elbow tiny.
And yet he is big now.
The one who came easily earth side
wide-shouldered and ready.
Steady, compassionate, easygoing.

I didn't know he was missing
till I met him and then I knew
we'd been waiting for him.
The one who showed me what I had become:
strong, aware, connected.

May 3, 2013

OUTSIDE

I arrive to pick them up from school.
I see them before they see me.

I recognize them
and at the same time they're not
the people I know at home.

I spend so much time thinking about them
when I see them far away from me
it's a shock.

They are completely outside me.

March 6, 2016

THE SIZE OF LOVE

Sometimes loving all of them feels too hard.
I don't know how to feel the whole size of it.
It's hard to love the part of them that fights me every day.
So I look at one small part.
The small soft tuft of hair where it meets the forehead.
The tip of the nose.
The curve of the shoulder.
I know how to love those places.
Those places love me back.
I smooth the hairline.
Gently tap the nose.
My palm on the shoulder,
its curve fills my hand.

My touch says, "I love you."
Some days loving the whole comes easy.
Some days I pour my intention, my love
into one small part
and hope my love spreads outward.
In loving the part, I love the whole.

I hope this synecdoche is enough.
A through line.
A touchstone.
A way to say, "I love you," even when it's hard.
A way to remind myself of my love even when loving is hard.
I hope on the days when I can't do it all
that part will be enough.

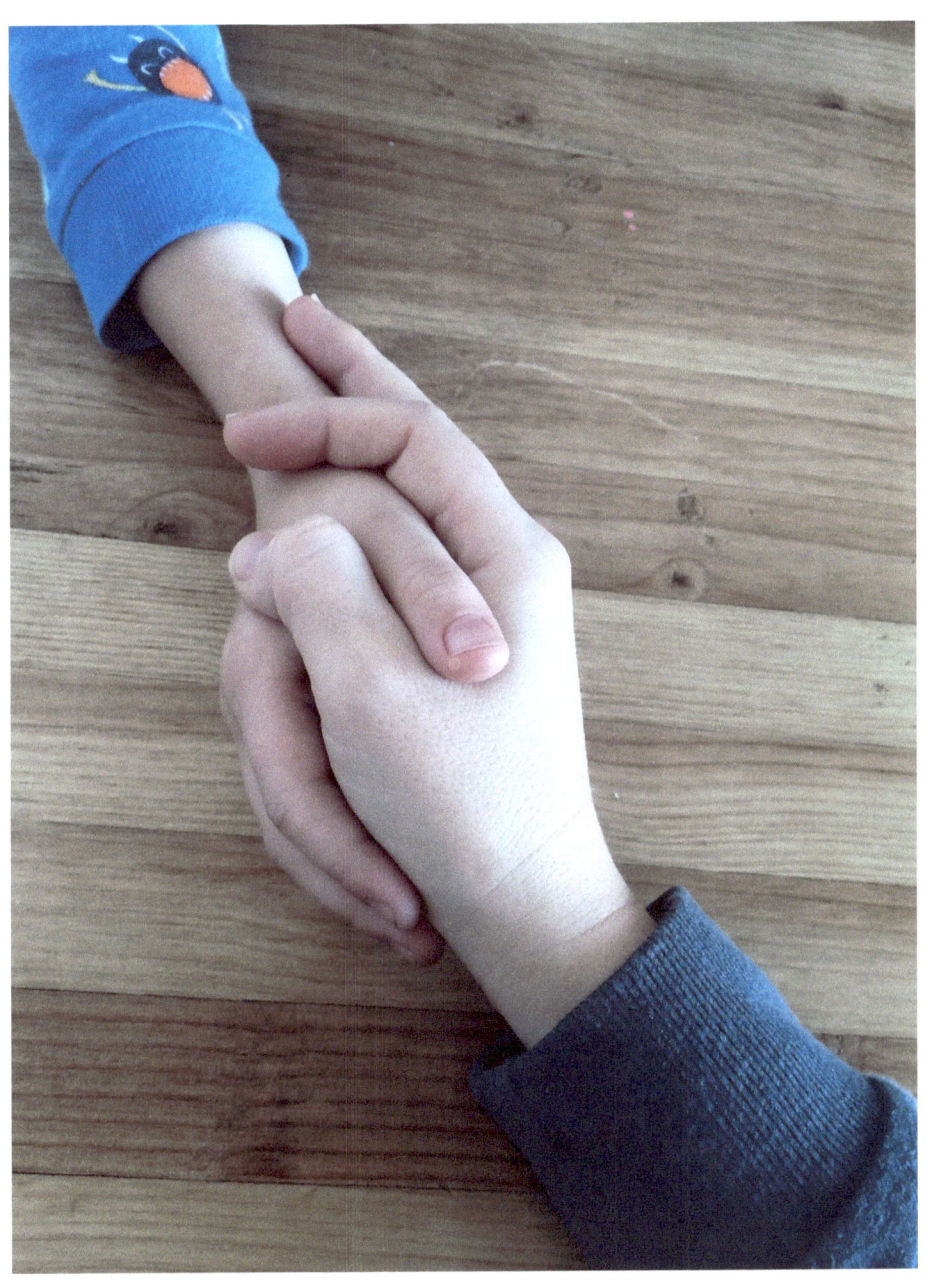

March 22, 2015

THE TIDE OF HER

Her body is changing.
She has so much to say.
Her mind jumps from subject to subject
before I catch the thread
of the first topic.

Every day she seeks out bigger responsibilities
yet refuses the commitments she already has.
She is walking desire for greatness
and doesn't want my help charting her path.
She wants to be a fashion designer, astronomer, astronaut, chemist,
and five other things besides.
As an adult, I know to gain mastery
you need to focus on one thing.
Commitment.
Depth.
But as her mom, I say,
"That's awesome baby!"
How does a mom encourage all the dreams
and at the same time encourage the focus
achieving even one of these dreams requires?

Parenting feels like a constant contradiction.
So many feelings
true at the same time.
So much conflicting advice.
Paralyzing.

And yet the tide of her rolls on
so I do the best I can.

I do not understand how she has gotten so big.
And yet, I can't remember her
as she was
when she was small.

Being bigger suits her.
Her want always outpaced her size.

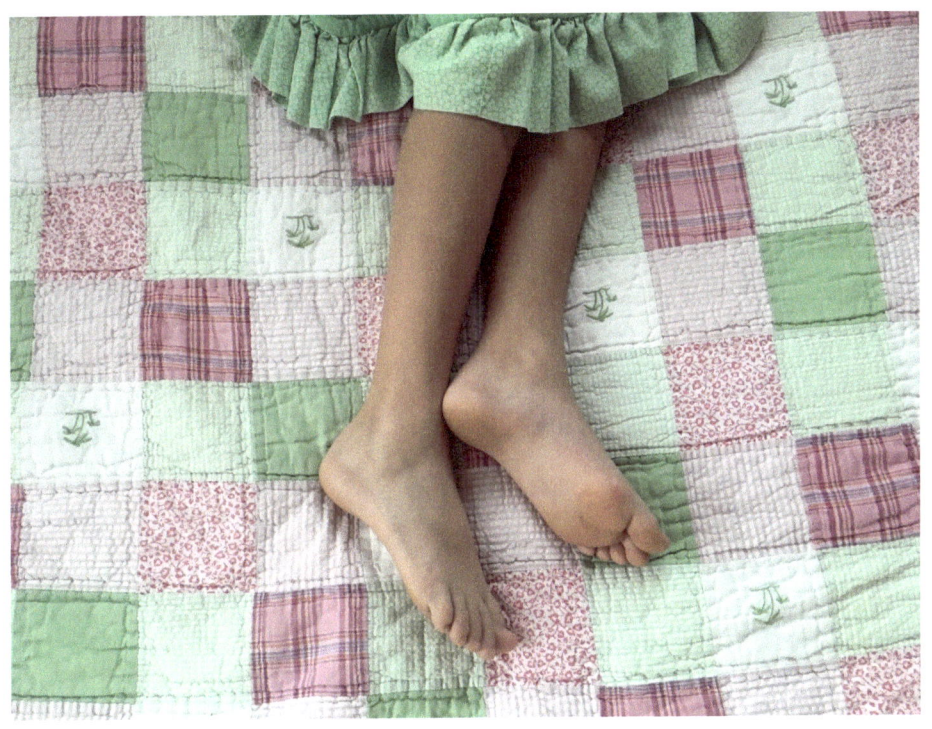

November 11, 2013

ALMOST DECADENT

My father was unconscious and unaware.
Or maybe that's too generous.
Maybe he knew he had a choice
and chose to do the things he did on purpose.

He was abusive.

I was abused.

It feels strange
and childish
and woe-is-me self-indulgent to say that.
There is something about saying those words straight up
that feels almost decadent to say out loud.
It doesn't feel good.
It feels like High Drama.
And I suppose it was.
He liked it that way.
But I didn't.
And I still don't.

I don't like saying it.
Having to say it.
Because yes, it was bad.
But I am ok.
It keeps coming up though.
Bubbling out.
I couldn't say it for so long
I have to say, claim it, now.
I don't want people to make up their own stories about what it means.
To put me and my life and what happened into a box
as if they already know
when I don't even know.

Key stories stand out. Moments that define.
The thing that hurt for so long was that
he hurt me
but I could never say exactly how
it hurt.
I could never say exactly what happened.
I'd come home sad, off, depleted, yucky.
Something *must* have happened.

I only knew having to be in his presence was a bad thing.

I am still afraid the walls I put in place are not enough
and he will find his way through
and hurt me again.
Though I can't imagine what could hurt more than the final hurt.

I am terrified I will become him,
suddenly lose control and do the unhealable.

I hate that though it's been fourteen years,
I still feel the exact pain and powerlessness.
The fear that a person can,
without warning,
turn into someone completely different.
Dangerous.

How do you tell the story of the things that happened to you
if you checked out while they happened to save yourself?

Again the dramatic hyperbole.

It's not like all that much actually happened.
A slap, a curse.
Yelling, yelling, yelling.
And the final straw.
The thing, once said, that can never be unheard.
I'm not repressing a Big Thing.
I've blurred over a thousand thousand small things.

And that's what makes this a hard story to tell.

How do you find the words to write about something
that is nothing really
and everything at all?

March 27, 2015

WITH A CAPITAL "A"

I haven't always taken up space.
I've tried to hide.
To numb out.
To disappear.
Waiting for someone else to come in and do it for me.
So much fear.

Yesterday I realized that all this time it's been Anxiety.
Looking back
I was afraid
to do almost everything.
Go into Chicago.
Travel on my own.
Sell my car.
Life was just barely possible.
Definitely not worth trying.
What if it didn't work?

My grandma let things be done unto her.
Even when she did travel,
everything was a disappointment.
It wasn't like it was back home.

I wouldn't ask.
I wouldn't assert or insist or demand.
Definitely never a demand.
Speak around things.
I thought I was being clear.
I really did.
I'd ask
and it wouldn't happen.
I couldn't say what I needed
because I didn't know what I needed.
I didn't know how to name it for myself.
I didn't have that skill.

I tried and tried and tried
in my own way
to get what I needed.
But I wasn't straightforward.
I wrapped what I needed inside other words.

Messages lost along the way.
My husband couldn't hear me.
So afraid to speak
but once in awhile it would all burst out
in a jumbled, accusatory mess.

Now I take up the right amount of space.
Advocate for myself when I need to.
Ask.
And expect to receive.
Do.
And expect it to work.
Refuse to back away and wish it off onto someone else.
Refuse to hide from myself.
Refuse to pretend I don't know
what I really want.
Know that I am capable.
Try, even if the outcome is unknown.
Make and keep promises to myself.
Believe that I am enough.

January 22, 2014

ENOUGH

The tape in my head runs over and over:
I'm not enough not enough not enough.
Every decision made without enough.

But what if I were already enough?
What would I do?

If my idea was already good enough,
how would I proceed?
If I were already creative enough,
what would I share?

If I were already a good enough mom,
what would I say
when she gets mad,
when he throws a fit,
when they want to play?

Let go of the tape, the constant
self-doubt, second-guessing, beating myself up.

Love myself through action.

It's not profound.
Right now is ok.
Nothing different than what already is.
It means believing I am already enough.
Past tense.
It has *already* happened.
Nothing to prove or earn
and already part of me.
Trust what I already know.
No explanation or preamble.
Show up
unfiltered.

Treat my family the same.
They are already enough too.
Nothing to fix.
Openhearted.

No longer paralyzed,
I'll know what is needed in the moment.
If I make a mistake,
I can make amends.
I can stop beating myself up with *better better better*.

They are mine.
I am the mom that they need.
Everything is already ok.

August 16, 2013

MATH PROBLEM

How do I let them be who they are?

They look right at me
and do the very thing they were asked not to.
They think underwear
belongs in the bookcase.
I'm rarely able to finish
a sentence
before their ideas burst out over mine.

As a parent, is it my job to control?
I want to.

Maybe all I need
is to be here.
Maybe they don't need my answers.
Maybe they need my questions more.

Is it really my job to shift things back to calm?
I want their anger to stop right now because I'm afraid.
I want it to stop by any means necessary.
I want to lash out.
Check out or barrel through.
Anything but staying here,
uncomfortable,
and so out of control.
I feel like a bad mom.
I should be better at this by now.
It makes me mad at the kids for not being "better" too.
If I were better,
I'd be able to control them.
If I could make them better,
I wouldn't have to.
The moment speeds up and everything feels right on top of me.

The opposite
would be to slow it all down,
pay more attention.
Stay right here.

What happens next?

I don't know.
I've already tried everything I can think of.
Nothing works.

What if my expectation is wrong?
Maybe it doesn't matter if I fix anything.
Maybe what matters is that they know
I am here with them
no matter what.
Maybe there is no way to know now
what I'll need to do then.
Maybe it's not to be premeditated.
I've expected it to be a script
or an if/then math problem.
If I do this one thing
or say this one thing
then I can make the anger disappear.

Maybe it's time for a new equation:
"This is hard,
I am here with you.
You're not alone.
We can figure it out."
Then see what happens next.

May 1, 2013

SURRENDER

She is my teacher.
I can't slack off around her.
She always calls on me,
even if I haven't raised my hand,
especially when she thinks I'm not paying attention.

She takes all my energy.
My full focus.
It feels so hard to give.
I've fought not to give myself over.
Can I give everything and trust
I will have at least something left of myself?
That more will be there when I need it?
Or do we both need to learn our boundaries?
She to not pull too hard?
And I to not bend too much?
Surrender, and what remains after surrender?

I thought I'd healed all my shit.
And then she was born.
Pokey in all the places I was tender.
So much about myself
I didn't know
that I didn't know.

I finally decided I would no longer be his whipping girl.
But I have to show up for her over and over again.
Though she is not him,
her panic response the same as his sudden,
irrational anger the
very thing I want to run from.
The thing that makes me go numb.
A useful survival skill when I was a kid.
Now I'm the parent.
My one job is to stay present.
So over and over again
I come right up to that tender edge.
Over and over again,

I practice not shutting down.
I am grateful
for her demanding spirit.

For long stretches of her early years
I couldn't back down from that ledge.
Terror rose
and I'd go over the edge
into powerless anger.
Living with a newborn,
the other shoe drops all day long.
It almost broke me.
It did break me.
I've spent the last ten years learning how to rebuild.
It is unfair I have to go through this again!
That once, as a child, wasn't enough.

Later. After a hard day.

I don't know what to do.
I don't know how to help her.
I don't know how to survive not being able to help.

She chooses to be upset.
She chooses to not let go, to let herself be helped.
She throws her feelings at me.
To not feel them herself.
I don't know how to withstand the attacks.
I don't know how to love her through her feelings.
I don't know how to do this for the rest of my life.

I shield my heart from her.
I suppose love would say
let that wall down.
Open your heart.
I try.
But I can't.
I will not be battered anymore.
Soften.
Not let her upset
upset me.
But I don't know how to do that either.

I am defeated.
I can't keep going.
I try.
But her rage overwhelms me.
I yell and yell and yell.
Becoming the thing I fear most.

It happens less often now that she is ten.
But every time she loses it
I am terrified I will be pulled down with her.
She is the only person who makes me feel this way.
I can't open my heart
I've been whacked so many times.
It breaks my heart
I can't seem to figure it out.
Stuck in a pattern I don't know how to unhook from.

February 9, 2013

LEARNING TO STAY

The thing itself is love. Love for them. Staying still.
Being. Looking. Hoping.
Returning back to the home. The heart.

My father didn't love me.
There was nothing for me
to return to.
I always tried to get away.
To get out and get gone.

But now, with them, I want to stay.
I don't want to check out.
So I don't.
I keep going.
I keep coming back again and again and again.

It's hard.
My habit is to leave, check out, get gone.

But here, there is love,
with and for them.
Something to return to,
a reason to stay.

That's what love is.
Staying.
Coming back.
Showing up.
Doubling down.
In abuse, to love yourself you have to leave them
to return to you. The self you'd lost
or quieted or stopped.

With love that's healthy, true, balanced,
it's the returning.
Making a mistake.
Yelling.
Checking out for a minute or a season. And then coming back.
Deeper each time.

Weaving together.

I am here.
I am staying.
Learning to say: *I am sorry.*

July 17, 2013

TWENTY YEARS

Twenty years from now she will be a few days shy of 30.
If she follows my path
and my mother's path,
she'll have a two-year-old.

I hope she will be ok.

The first two years of her life were hard for me.
Hopefully twenty years from now the pain will have faded
or become ever more fruitful.
I hope it won't be so hard for her.
I hope she will have help.
I hope she will know how to ask for what she needs.
I hope she and her partner feel like they're on the same team,
working through whatever comes, together.
I hope she has an identity beyond kids.
More than "just a mom."
Something to call her own.
Science. Inventions. Engineering.
What might she design to make the world better and more beautiful for all of us?
I can't imagine how she will change the world.
But *she* can.

He will be 27.
So old and yet so young.
A pattern of his whole life so
big and so small at the same time.
If he follows his father's path
he'll have been married for two years and dreaming about kids.
He wants to build houses
to make things with his hands.
I can't wait to see what his tender heart will build.
Maybe he will build a house for us.
To live in a house built by my son.

And in 20 years he will be dead.
There's no way he's making it to 98.

And I will be free.
Sometimes I imagine cinematic reconciliations.
Sometimes I imagine I am strong enough
to have him in my life when he's feeling well
and to hold the boundary when he turns.

But why?
There is nothing to gain from the well times
that wouldn't hurt doubly taken away by the turning.
I don't have the room for an unreliable resource.

In twenty years, perhaps sooner, I will be able to return home
without fearing the bogeyman.
I won't always have to hold some part of my brain poised
for what if.
The other shoe will finally have dropped
and it will be ok.

February 27, 2013

MY JOB

I don't want to write from his point of view
or stand in his gross shoes.
I don't really care why he did what he did
or whatever excuse he makes up
to make me the bad guy.
I do feel empathy
but it's external.
I tried for years to make sense of it.
To understand.
To figure out why.
Contorted myself for years
to mean enough to him to make him see
past his own lens.
If he loved me enough he would stop.
If I could be enough
I could inspire him to stop.
But I wasn't enough.

So I practice being enough for them
enough for myself.
I worry
I'm messing them up.
Repeating the pattern.
My greatest fear.
But when I look through their eyes
I see their love for me.
They see me trying
every moment
of every day
to love them.
To truly love them.
To love them through their own eyes
and not through mine.
And in that way I can see
that through the trying
I become enough.
In their eyes
I don't have to be different.
I just have to be me

and love them.
They look at me with love.
I am grateful.

My job is
to come back to them
again
again
again
so that they can see me with love.
They say that love is blind.
But they are wrong.
Love sees.
And they see me with love.
It is enough.
It is the healing blessing.
To know I have stopped the cycle.

May 11, 2013

ALREADY FORGIVEN

There was another way I could have played it.
In the middle of everything I could have shut down, armored up.
Impossible to reach my heart.
I went the other way.
Stayed broken open.

My mom.
As much as he couldn't see, she always did.
Always there. Constant. Open.
Seeing me clearly.
Already forgiven when I am at my worst.
She showed me what love looks like.
The direction to head.
She was the first step in breaking the cycle.
She couldn't walk away for herself.
But she walked away,
kept us safe,
because of me.
For her I was always enough.
For her, I *never have* to.
For me, she was willing to do the hardest thing.
Leave.
She doesn't always see what she can be,
but she sees me.
I put words to what she couldn't see,
and together we heal.

April 23, 2011

EVIDENCE

I am still afraid of making you mad
so I haven't spoken the truth to you.
I am afraid of you.
It's not just that I don't trust you,
and let's be clear,
I absolutely don't trust you.
I am also afraid of you.
I don't want to be around you or see your face.
When I see people who look like you,
I jolt in fear.
I triple check
to prove to myself
it isn't you.

I wish I could prove to you
that what you did was wrong.
I'm hung up on it.
It's so tempting —
the idea that if I wrote you
I could make you see
my side.
You never will.
If you could have,
you couldn't have kept doing what you did.

Emotional abuse leaves no physical evidence.
It's hidden, unnamable, invisible.
It was a long time before I called it abuse.
I still ask myself if it's really what happened.
But it is.
I hate you for the fear, doubt, and anxiety you've caused me.
I hate how I still pull out shrapnel from you.
I hate what you did to my mom
and how small she still feels
because you made her believe that she was nothing.
You tried to make me believe that I was nothing too.
I believed you for a long time.
I don't believe you any more.

I prove it to myself.
But I can't prove it to you.
I can't make you see.
I can't make you see me for who I really am.

But I can see other people.
Bring out the best in them.
Show them how special they are.
So they know.
So they believe me.
I photograph the moments as proof,
a reminder if they forget.

It's true, I have pictures of us that look like proof of love too.
But I didn't consent to those pictures.
When you look at those pictures, look at my eyes.
Starting at a very early age
you can tell
I don't want to be there.
And it's more than just being a cranky teenager.
You made sure I had no will when you were around.

On visitation days
we followed your plan.
I'm sure you told yourself
you did it all for me.
But you alone made the decisions.
I know kids don't always get to choose.
But you dominated
every aspect
of every movement.
And now
I think it's dangerous to want things.
I feel ineffective.
I am afraid of taking up space.

I try to prove it to myself.
To understand it was real.
It is still so hard for me to believe it.
But my body doesn't lie.
The last time I went home, a wrong turn took us close to your house.

My whole body screamed,
Run!

That was my proof.
My mind is unsure.
But my body knows.
You are unsafe.
My body only responds that way to you.
No.
I do not excuse you
because your parents hurt you.
You could have tried
to be different if you wanted to.
I work to be a better parent.
I second-guess
every move I make because of you.

There is no love for you
or from you
in my heart.
Only the need to defend.
What you did
was not love.
I think your name,
and my heart slams shut.
You do not belong there.

October 2, 2015

CHRISTMAS MORNING

It's hard to describe how it feels to say,
"I was emotionally abused."
It is raising your hand in class,
but you're not sure your answer is right,
so you say it really fast
and hope no one notices.
How can this really be the right answer?

It is being afraid I'll have to defend my answer
and not know how.
That I will say,
"I was abused."
and the Prosecution will respond,
"Oh, yeah? Prove it."

How can it be true?
I had no visible scars.
No broken bones, belt marks, or burns.

What if I am wrong?
What if he did love me?
Does love me?
But he's so broken that it comes out all wrong.

When I was with him I was broken.
There was no me left.
No presents on Christmas morning.
Threats of suicide
but everything was fine when the cops came.
The ground, unsteady.
The landscape always changing.

It happened.
My brain makes excuses.
Trying to make it not real.
Oh it wasn't as bad as it could have been.
Because I can't believe it was as bad as it was.

It happened.
I was abused.

And now when I say it,
it feels a little like pride.
Like presents on Christmas morning.
Like truth.
Like survival.

June 28, 2014

IT LOOKS NOTHING LIKE I THOUGHT IT WOULD

I was terrified to marry my husband.

I didn't see it coming.
The proposal,
the answer.

The terror.

I didn't see any of it coming.
We'd only been together nine months.
Had talked around marriage as a romantic notion
but never head-on
as a practically reality.

He had the video camera running.
I decide the future as he waits on bent knee.
Close my eyes and ask the question silently of myself.

Would I?
yes
Really?
YES

I said yes out loud.

On some days, for some years,
that internal yes that is the only reason I remain.
That voice.
I didn't know I had that voice.
A clear, simple, strong yes.
Even when I felt like he definitely wasn't on my side,
even when it seemed like he must definitely be working against me,
I took refuge in that one small word.
Even as panic tightened my chest,
I knew the word yes came from somewhere deeper.
I trusted it even when I couldn't trust myself.

I trust it was right then and it is right now.
"How did you know he was *The One*?"
they ask in the movies.
"Oh, I just knew," they answer,
as if there was never any doubt.

In that first moment I just knew too.

But then the doubt. The fear. This couldn't be right.
It had only been one month since I had stopped speaking to my dad.
We changed the date. And then changed it again. And a third time.
Horror stories of women not realizing they'd made a mistake till they're walking down the aisle.
How could I know if that would be me?

I lost friends
who thought I was rushing too quickly.
They were right.
I didn't know how to slow down,
so I cut them out instead.

My mom didn't know how to fit
into a large family
so she held on tighter.
She had always been my one and only
and I didn't know how to grow
love to include more than just us.

We fought.
I didn't know who I was anymore.
I couldn't believe someone could love me
so I made myself as unlovable as possible
assumed the worst intentions.

I thought I was the only one.
Every movie ever made said this was supposed to be
the happiest time of my life.
If things went wrong, they were to do so in campy Hollywood style.

How could someone like me stay forever?
Did I want to be with him tomorrow? Yes.
And tomorrow? Yes.

And after that? Yes.
But how do those yeses add up to forever?
What is the difference between
fear of the unknown
and making a huge mistake?

I didn't know fear
does not always mean
shut down
run away.
I didn't know fear also means
wake up
pay attention
show up
use your voice
this matters
participate.

I moved forward anyway.
Put on the dress.
Walked down the aisle
to this man
and said our vows.
He forgot his lines.
I pointed out the mistake, like a jerk.
I overacted my vows, like a jerk.
Each word emphasized and pronounced
so that the audience would get it.
Was I trying to convince myself?

We got married.
The world didn't end.

I wanted to do it all again the next day
so I could be myself.
We've been married 13 years this August.
I know now
what the words I said then
truly mean.
I found my voice.
He stays every day.
I stay every day.
It looks nothing like I thought it would

I finally let him love me.

I stop telling the story, "I was dragged into this."
I stop telling the story, "I didn't choose this."

Yes.

This is the life I chose.
This is the life I choose.

May 30, 2014

GROWING UP

I wonder what it would be like if I'd never had them.
Easier.
But I wouldn't have any way of knowing the difference.
I wouldn't have done the hard work of growing into a mother.
Having never done that, I would never know the pain I would have
passed over.
I would have grown differently, twisted in a different direction
by the light of a different sun.

I wasn't sure I wanted to be a mom.
It seemed like the right thing to do at the time.
I hadn't yet felt the longing in my heart.
I wasn't ready.
No one ever is.
I was even less ready than that.
I didn't know how to stand firmly on my own feet yet.
How to take up the space of my own life.
I was not ready to take responsibility for someone else's.

When I told my mother I was pregnant she went silent.
Having been a mom for 27 years at that point, she knew what I did not.
But she could not say.

I chose to have him.
It took two years to decide.
I wasn't ready to be a mom again,
to risk a return of post partum anxiety.
Then one night,
listening to a friend sing under the stars,
I looked up
and knew I was ready.
I chose him.

Can I now choose her?
Instead of saying
I don't want to,
I don't know how to,
I wish it hadn't happened,
I wish it were different,

I wish she was different,
can I choose it all?
It's certainly not what I would have chosen.
I didn't expect the pain of having to grow up alongside her.

But can I choose her now,
just as she is,
not long for a different reality,
but open my heart and choose this one?
Stand up and fight for it.
Double down and commit.
Fierce in my acceptance?

Yes.

October 17, 2013

HOLD US BOTH

I wish I could go back
to take care of me then.
Offer myself a hand back through time.
Give myself the words to ask for the help I needed.
I wish I'd known I didn't have to be alone under the waves.

I wish I could go back and give myself a sense of peace.
The ability to let myself rest.
I wish I could have known your cries were not criticisms.
Each and every one only ever meant, "Love me. Feed me."
Full stop.
No other meaning.

I wish I could parent you with a stronger heart.
Love you with my fullness
rather than the battered and bruised broken pieces.
I wish you the strength in your voice it took me these years to find.

I wish I could go back and hold us both
hold the panic at bay so that we could rest
in the peace between the need.
I wish we could be easy with each other.

I got pregnant the very first time we tried.
I was not ready for the reality of you.
From the moment you were born,
bright red and screaming,
you made me work hard
way past the strength I thought I had.

The only thing I can do is give us peace now.
Abide in the lull
rather than bracing for the next wave.
It's coming
whether I like it or not.
And I can love you fiercely now
to make up for the ways I couldn't then.

I love you.

You said, "I wish I could say I love you all day long
so that you know I love you all the time."
Or something like that.
I should have written it down.

You know with your whole being
that I love you with my whole being.
The anger is on the surface.
We are enough for each other.
Our anger doesn't mean our love comes and goes.

His did.
He did not love me well.
His rage made love conditional.

Our anger says, "I love you. Help me."
Our love is not intermittent.

September 22, 2009

GOOD

I am happy.
I look for reasons to doubt it.
To disprove it's really how I feel.
But I am happy.
Now.
I chose them.
I chose myself.
I'm not running away,
looking for a savior
or a way out
any more.
I'm here.
Committed
to myself
and to them.
I have what it takes.

Right now it's darn good.
Now is not then.
What I experienced becomes
what I have learned
which has become who I am.

I am proud of this person.
I am proud.

To wish the past away
is to wish this person away.

They say to figure out what you want to do with your life
think back to what you wanted to be as a kid.
But what I want now
is the thing I *didn't* want then.
I didn't want to be unseen.
I didn't want to be negated.
I didn't want to be silenced.
What I want now is to see,
recognize,
speak.

So much time spent living what I did not want
taught me to look beyond and underneath and around
to see the hidden pattern.
What's really going on.
A gift.

When my kids look at me
all I see is their love.
We're doing the normal fall and rise of family life.
I am honest with them.
I pray they know how hard I try.

I write the story from the middle now.
Shaping the meaning toward home.
I struggle with every word that leaves my mouth.
Hoping it heals instead of hurts.

May 22, 2011

THROUGH LINE

We always come back to each other.
We have hard moments.
We are not our best.
We let each other down.

We renew and return.
We wake up in the morning.
We are new
and start again.

It's how I know we're ok.

December 27, 2012

WHAT WORKS

Remember:
What works for me
doesn't always work for her.

She is her own person,
separate from me.
Several steps beyond my reach.

I watch from afar
and wonder
at the distance between us.

She is of me,
loved by me,
and yet so far away.
So much I don't understand.
Even when I think I do,
I don't know what's going on in her mind,
her heart.

Do not assume
the pattern
is predictable.

She is not me.

I slow down.
Look. Wait.
Willing to be surprised.
Ask what she needs.
Let her choose
even when hers is different
from mine.

Let her grow.

January 22, 2016

QUIET

He is joy and tenderness.
A quiet place to rest.
We are quiet together.
He doesn't need me
to be any different
than I am.

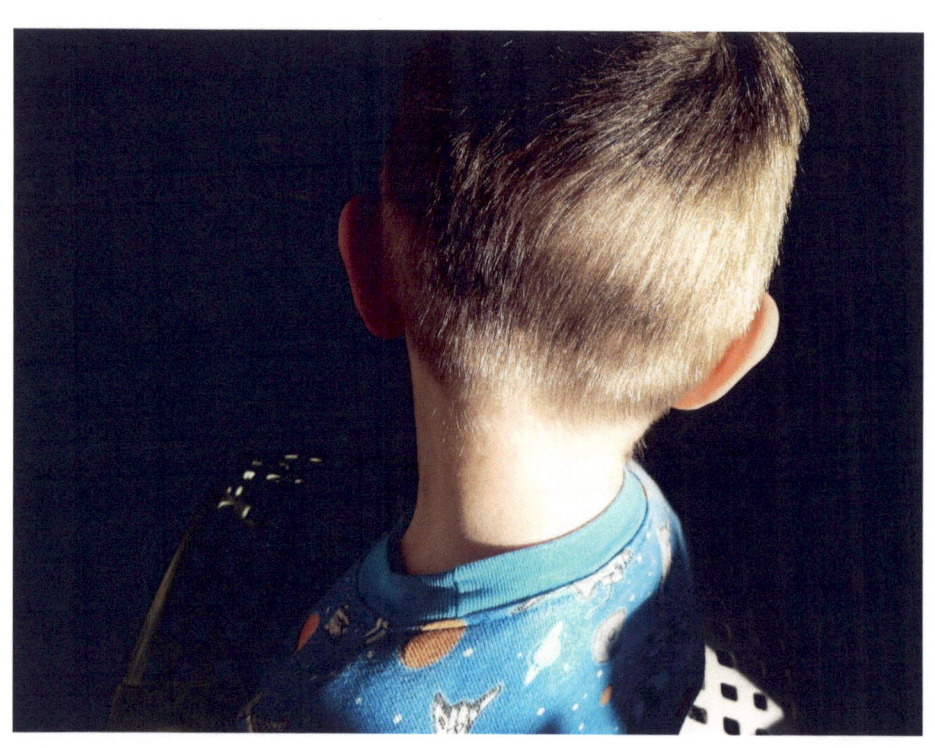

January 12, 2013

ELEMENTAL

"Huggie Mommy!"
Her body collapses on mine.
His on top of hers.
Hers on top of me.
They try to push closer and closer.
Push the other one out of the way.
Push closer into me.
If you could push through my very skin, you would.

I suck at nighttime snuggles.
Come bedtime
I really just want them to go away.
No amount of cute hugs
doesn't feel like stalling.
It doesn't feel like love at night.
I want to push away.
Just one more, mom. Just one more, mom. Just one more.
It doesn't feel like truth. It feels like desperation.
I haven't done enough. They haven't gotten enough.
Another day I've let them down.
Another time I chose the quiet over them.
Morning snuggles, on the other hand.
Starting the day off quiet
I climb in bed next to you.
I smooth your hair.
Check your ears for gunk,
a habit from when you used to fall asleep in my arms.
Your still-thin
arms reach around my neck
as they've done for seven years. Ten years.
Warm. Skin warm. Heart warm.
I like you more in the morning.
We are all full of promise. Groggy, but more elemental.
Not the story of you,
or the story of me,
or how we've come together
or failed each other throughout the day.
Just us.
Together.

June 28, 2014

HAIRBRUSH

I brush your hair
as you eat your raisin bran
half naked.

Your hair is short now.
Easier to brush.
A giant snarl sticks out in back.
I separate the strands.
Gently gently.
Smooth my hand over your head
with each pass of the brush.
Loving you through my palms.

Your hair is dirty.
You need a shower.
The strands stick together as I brush.
I don't say anything.
Nothing good could come from it.
Nothing to be done about it now anyway.
I am trying not to criticize.
Bite my tongue.
Tell you only what is useful.
Or kind.
You can shower later even though I know you hate it.
Maybe today, rainy and cold,
is a good day for a bath.

I keep my mouth shut.
And just brush.
Brush.
Stroke.
Smooth.
Loving you through my palms.
Hoping you feel it.
Hoping you know.

Sometimes words get in the way between us.
You and I, we both love words.
We have a lot to say.

Want to be heard.
Sometimes we have so many words
that we talk past each other.
Words words words going out.
Little coming in.

So I love you through my palms
and hope you know
I will brush your hair forever
and always love you.

July 19, 2014

ONE THIN ARM

Early January.
Still full dark.
Even now it's hard to wake the sleeping baby.
But it's a school day.
So, my little boy.
My son my son.
I jiggle you gently.
Roll over little man, my little guy.
Seven and a half.
So big and still so small.

Eyes closed, you open your mouth.
I pour in the powder.
Grateful for its help.
It does seem to get you out of your own way,
let the best parts of you shine through.
Shorten the path so you can find the right words.
And you, like your sister and I, have so many words.
Twenty when one will do.
I am grateful for how it helps you.
And worried at what cost this straight path comes.
Are we hurting in our efforts to help?
I have to believe that we are not.
That this is the right choice.
That all will be well, and all will be well, and all will be well.
And yet with each capsule I also offer a little prayer.

You drink from the tiny A&W mug.
Just enough to get your medicine down.
Eyes still closed.
You grimace slightly as you swallow.
But every morning you take it.
You never fight.
Never roll over, clamp your mouth shut, and straight out refuse.
And it gives me hope, that you feel it helps.
You notice a difference in how you experience the world.
And you like the way it feels.
And not the opposite, that your trust in us is so complete,
you'd take it no matter what, just because we said so.

You lay back down,
fold yourself deeper under the blanket,
then shoot out one thin arm
and grab me around the neck.
We pull each other close.
You still fit into the curve of me.
Your arm almost reaches around my neck.

We don't need words.
We have always been able to be quiet with each other.
You breathe your morning hitch-breath.
You don't breathe like this any other time.

We hold each other close.
You want to be right up next to me.
And I with you.
We rest there together.
Sure of each other
as we wait to fully wake up.

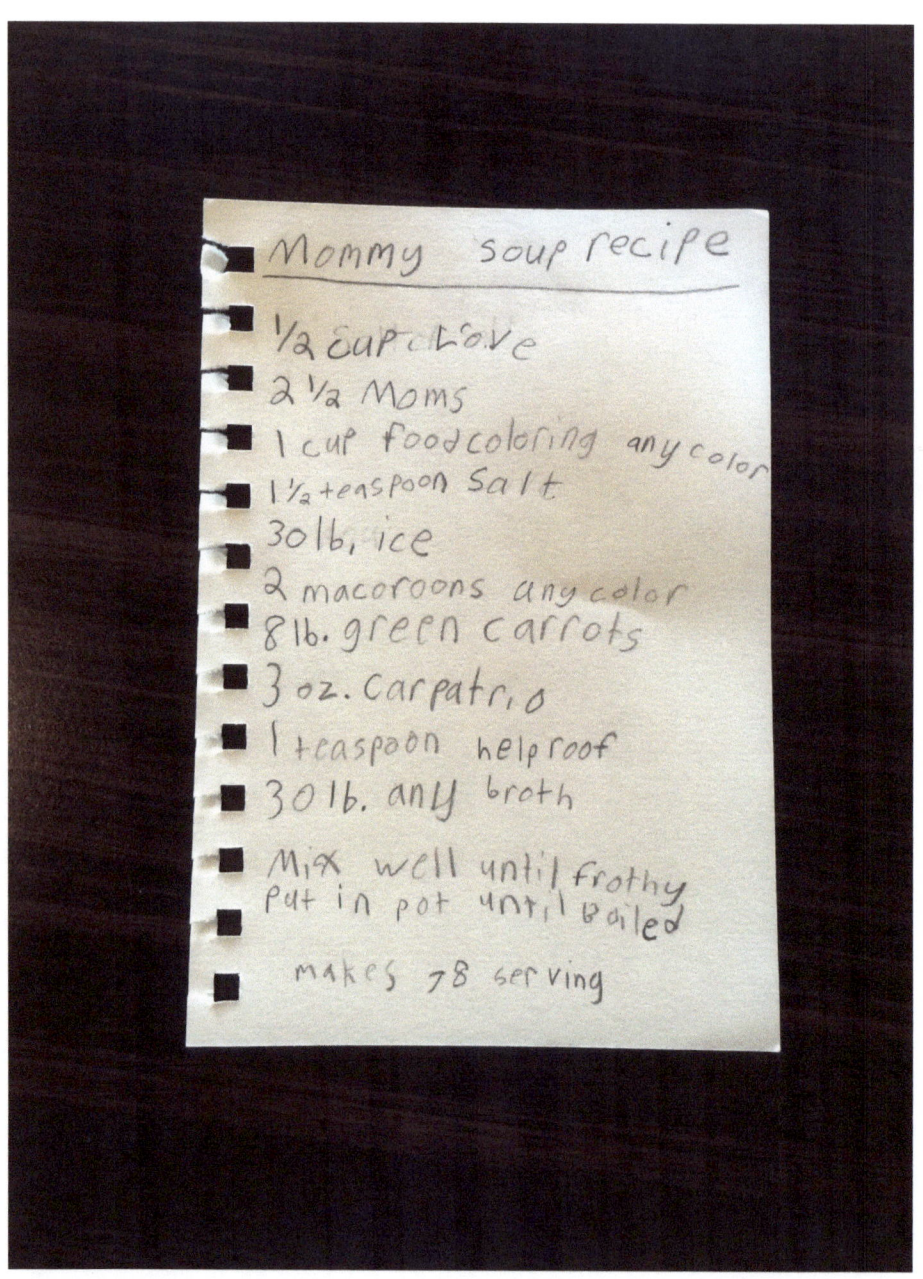

March 22, 2015

PRACTICE

I see you both growing.
Not every day.
But all at once.

We drive home from a party
and you are quiet the whole way home.
You play without fighting.
Sometimes.
You play on your own.
You don't need me to keep you from eating sand or rocks or candy you swiped off some kid.
You ride the carousel on the other side of the park by yourself.
I can't see you from where I sit.
You watch tv in the other room while I write.
You don't need me every single second.

I send you off into the world,
a little ways off,
and you do just fine.

We learn to trust each other in new ways.
You trust me to come back.
I trust you to come back.
You go to the park wearing my watch
and you come back on time.
You know how to cross the street.
You know how to play on the playground equipment
without killing yourselves.
You watch out for each other.
You know how to trust your gut
and how to ask for help if I'm not there.
You are where you say you're going to be.
Most of the time.
You come back.
We practice you growing up.
I practice letting go.
You practice the complex tasks of going.

I hope when you have a choice to make
you act from the home place in your heart.
I hope you always want to come home.

October 9, 2015

HALF

It's my half birthday.
I am thirty eight and a half.
My mom remembers.
She can't remember if the drug store is called CVS or CSV
but she always knows me by my name.

Sometimes I'm wretched and she loves me anyway.
She listens as I talk and talk and talk.
She makes me feel like I hung the moon.
She is steadfast, constant, unending.
She offers everything up to me,
everything that matters.
Her time
her energy
her undivided attention
her love.
The Giving Tree.

I don't want to be that boy.
I don't want to take and take and take
till there's nothing left of her.
I want to give back, nourish, add on.
So she can stay with us forever.

I will be wildly undone when she goes.
Nobody knows the bones of me the way she does.
She made them.

I go into the world because she is there.
I keep going because she believes in me.

January 22, 2016

NAME IT

Now that I name it,
call it emotional abuse.
Or just abuse.
Now that I say,
It happened,
I bring it into my heart.
I stop grappling with the reality of it.
I stop denying it.
I bring the small, young, scared part of me
into my heart
and love her there.
Knowing I've survived is a special secret.
A good secret.
It makes me powerful.
Strong. Hopeful.
Like Christmas morning
when you know something good is on its way.

June 24, 2016

MAGIC

I love him.

For safety
and time
and the steadfast foundation.

Here
as I grow up
and become
myself.

I didn't scare him away.
He didn't try to keep me small.
He grows too.

We are in it together
now
after fifteen years
in a way that we weren't
even a year ago.

For us
the magic is in staying,
becoming
more and more ourselves.

April 23, 2011

MOSTLY OK

I worry less now
about whether or not I am a good mom.
I am mostly ok most of the time.
It snuck up on me.
I no longer fall asleep reviewing all the ways I failed.
I am fluid now
not constantly paralyzed
or terrified I'm doing it all wrong.

I don't know what changed.
They know me.
They see me.
I know them.
I see them.

I feel it.
And they feel it.
I don't have the energy to worry about perfection any more.
I used to try so hard it hurt.
Not now.
Now I just want to be here with them.

May 24, 2012

FOR SURE

I don't know if I will be able to keep going.
And yet, in my heart, I do.

I love you.
I know that for sure.

I don't know if I can forgive myself.
And yet, in my heart, I do.

I love you.
I know that for sure.

I don't know what I'm doing.
And yet, in my heart, I do.

I love you.
I know that for sure.

I am afraid.
And yet, in my heart, I am not.

I love you.
I know that for sure.

I don't know how to trust myself.
And yet, in my heart, I do.

I love you.
I know that for sure.

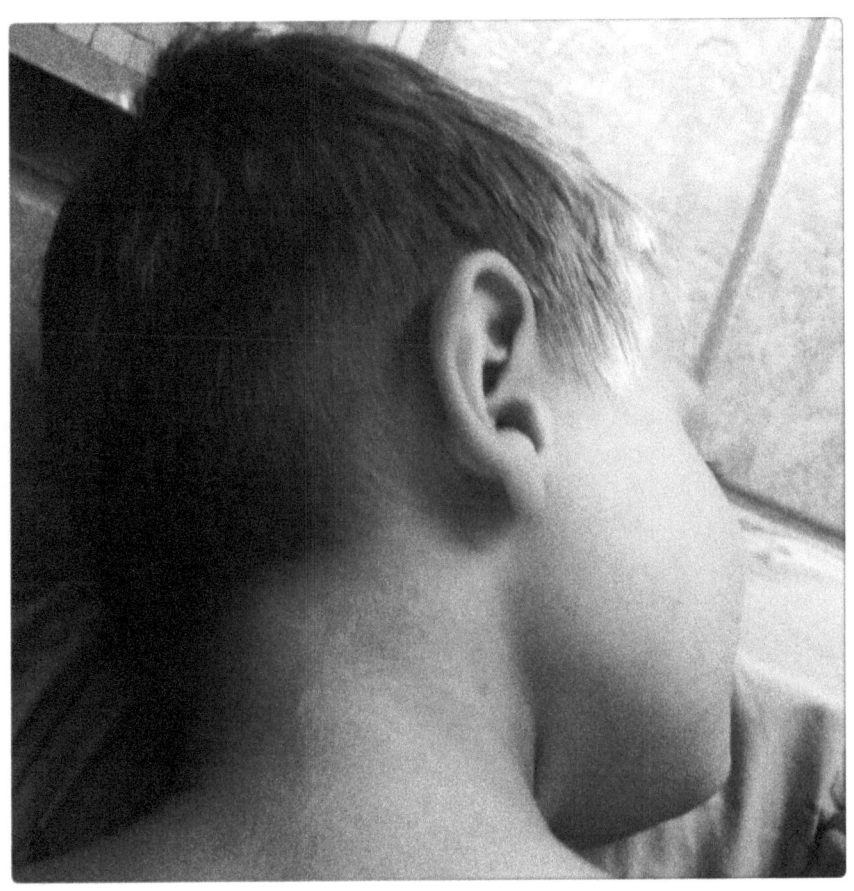

September 7, 2012

NO OTHER SHOE

We are safe.
The cycle broken,
no other shoe waiting to drop.

I have survived.

Whatever comes next
I'll survive it too.
I am strong enough.

December 15, 2012

AFTERWARD

Unbeknownst to me at the time, my dad died the same weekend I printed out the first draft of this book.

It was unexpected. And at the same time I'd been bracing for it for years. When I found out he was gone, I was relieved.

Our relationship was many things but it was not typical. For most of my life he was drowning in his mental illness. He could not see me clearly through it. And I never really got to experience the man I have heard stories about and know him to have been before I was born.

The way his illness manifested made him unpredictable. He had periods of stability and then would lash out in sudden and, to my child self, unpredictable explosions of anger. I think, by the time I came along, maybe his efforts to control the swings by himself made him monolithic in his efforts to control absolutely everything about me. He only slapped me once but I was always afraid of him.

When I was 24, I asked him to stop. I asked him to not call me for a month. He called me a "fucking bitch." He called my mother and threatened to kill himself. When the police arrived at his house he was totally fine. But that was the beginning of the end for me. He called me two days later. He harassed me at work. These calls were not tender or remorseful. These calls were mean. Manipulative. There were more suicide threats. I changed my number. Quit my job. Moved states.

By the time I began writing this book, I hadn't spoken to him in fourteen years.

And now he is gone.

My first year at college in Chicago, he came out to visit for parents' weekend. He took me to REI to buy me my first winter coat. Being from Hawai'i, neither of us knew what we were doing. We thought bigger must be better so we bought a blue coat in a size men's extra large tall. The salesperson must have thought it was for my dad and not for me or he would've never let us leave with such a ridiculous item of clothing. The wind would whip up and into that thing, puffing me out like a freezing balloon. My friends called me Babe the Blue Ox.

Before he moved back to Hawaiʻi from LA, he drove out to Chicago to give me his car. It was also blue inside and ridiculously too large for me—a 1990 Ford Crown Victoria with fog lights and a white leather roof. It was a bitch to park and fishtailed all over the snow. My friends called it my penis car, because it was the car of a 60-year-old man, not a 20-year-old girl.

He loved movies and books and all things radio. He took me to see *When Harry Met Sally* and *A Fish Called Wanda*. He introduced me to *The Godfather*.

He loved the main branch of the Honolulu Public Library. He got me my first library card and we spent hours in the stacks doing research and looking for the next good book.

He loved pulling elaborate pranks with and on his friends. In true Hawaiian style, they all became my aunties and uncles.

He loved Elvis and John F. Kennedy.

He loved Hawaiʻi. He taught me how to say the state motto and the state fish. Hawaiʻi Ponoʻī always made him cry.

I do believe that there was a part of him that loved me as best he could. And I am sad that that part was so often distorted through his illness. I do wish that it could have been different.

I do not regret my choice. I revisited it many times over the years. Wondering if I had healed enough, or if I was strong enough to tell when he was in his wellness and when he was in his sickness. I received calls on my business number. Emails. All threatening. Never once did he say, "I love you. I miss you. I don't know what happened, but I'm sorry." And so each time I decided that I was strong enough to stay away.

But he has also been right here with me this whole time. He is why I love a good story. Why I find myself drawn to radio. Why I can sense other people's moods and feelings so clearly. Why I am the loudest person in the room when I'm excited. He had a true knack for what was compelling, what made people pay attention. This is something I cherish in myself.

He also is why I work every moment and meditate every day to control my own anger. To grapple with my fierce desire to control my own kids. He is why I have the honor to say that Hawai'i is my home. And now I can finally go back.

I would not change what happened. It shaped who I am. Pain became strength. And I honor him for that. I know he was suffering. I know my decision caused him great pain. I pray that now he knows why. I pray that now he is released. And now that he is gone, I am free to share my story with you.

WHY 38?

I was 38 when I wrote these poems. 38 just happened to be the right number of poems to tell this story. My husband proposed to me on 3/8, which also happens to be International Women's Day. And the day they found my father's body. I didn't know any of this at the time. I only pulled the pieces together at the end when I was searching for a title for this book. Once I saw the pattern, I knew 38 had to be the title.

ACKNOWLEDGEMENTS

Thank you to Jena Schwartz and Janelle Hanchett for your amazing writing classes, without which I wouldn't have known I needed to write a memoir, I wouldn't have known these needed to be poems, and I wouldn't have found my way to these words.

Thank you Melissa Black, Sarah Bray, Julie Daley, Andrea Lewicki, and Sutton Long my mentors, guides, colleagues, and friends in art. Thank you for asking the questions, sharing your feedback, offering the support, and walking with me on the path. An extra debt of gratitude goes out to Sutton Long for the gift of laying out and designing this manuscript. Without your impeccable eye and wild talent this book literally wouldn't exist.

Thank you to Tessa, Mallory, Jen, Káren, and Illana who love me for who I am, honestly and gently guide me back when I lose my way, and hold the space for me to practice saying the raw vulnerable truth out loud.

Thank you to my family Kiki, Joe, Renée, Max, Bonnie, Neil, and Danielle for absolutely everything. You are my heart. Without you, nothing works.

ABOUT THE AUTHOR

Miki DeVivo is a writer and photographer committed to using art and story to change the cultural expectation of parental perfection. Making space for more stories means more room to be who we are, see ourselves clearly, and love more fully. For more stories and information, and to join the Parenting Out Loud community, please visit www.mikidevivo.com.

www.ingramcontent.com/pod-product-compliance
Lightning Source LLC
Chambersburg PA
CBHW042339150426
43195CB00006B/110